ARIZONA

The Grand Canyon State

BY
JOHN HAMILTON

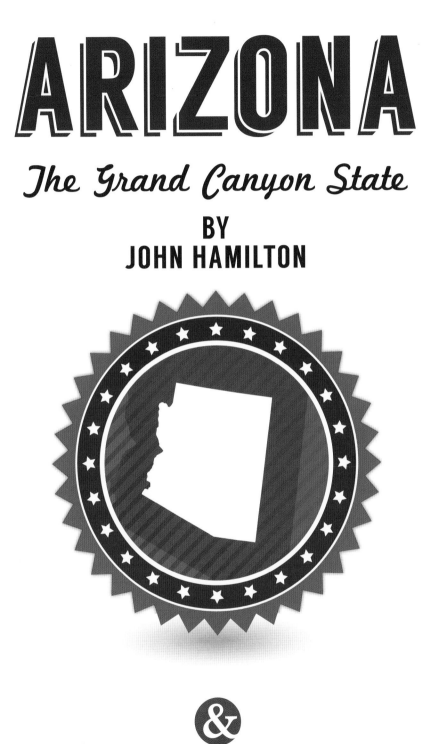

Abdo & Daughters

An imprint of Abdo Publishing | abdopublishing.com

abdopublishing.com

Published by ABDO Publishing, a division of ABDO, PO Box 398166, Minneapolis, Minnesota 55439. Copyright © 2017 by Abdo Consulting Group, Inc. International copyrights reserved in all countries. No part of this book may be reproduced in any form without written permission from the publisher. ABDO & Daughters™ is a trademark and logo of ABDO Publishing.

Printed in the United States of America, North Mankato, Minnesota.
012016
092016

Editor: Sue Hamilton   **Contributing Editor:** Bridget O'Brien
Graphic Design: Sue Hamilton
Cover Art Direction: Candice Keimig   **Cover Photo Selection:** Neil Klinepier
Cover Photo: iStock
Interior Images: Alamy, AP, Arizona Cardinals, Arizona Coyotes, Arizona Diamondbacks, Arizona Rattlers, Arizona United SC, Corbis, Dreamstime, Jon Gittins, Getty, Glow Images, Granger, History in Full Color Restoration/Colorization, iStock, Library of Congress, Mile High Maps, Mountain High Maps, National Archives, One Mile Up, Phoenix Mercury, Phoenix Suns, U.S. Congress, U.S. Dept. of Transportation, U.S. Postal Service, Wikimedia.

Statistics: *State and City Populations*, U.S. Census Bureau, July 1, 2014 estimates; *Land and Water Area*, U.S. Census Bureau, 2010 Census, MAF/TIGER database; *State Temperature Extremes*, NOAA National Climatic Data Center; *Climatology and Average Annual Precipitation*, NOAA National Climatic Data Center, 1980-2015 statewide averages; *State Highest and Lowest Points*, NOAA National Geodetic Survey.

Websites: To learn more about the United States, visit booklinks.abdopublishing.com. These links are routinely monitored and updated to provide the most current information available.

Cataloging-in-Publication Data

Names: Hamilton, John, 1959- author.
Title: Arizona / by John Hamilton.
Description: Minneapolis, MN : Abdo Publishing, [2016] | The United States of
 America | Includes index.
Identifiers: LCCN 2015957504 | ISBN 9781680783056 (print) | ISBN
 9781680774092 (ebook)
Subjects: LCSH: Arizona--Juvenile literature.
Classification: DDC 979.1--dc23
LC record available at http://lccn.loc.gov/2015957504

CONTENTS

The Grand Canyon State 4

Quick Facts 6

Geography 8

Climate and Weather 12

Plants and Animals. 14

History. 18

Did You Know? 24

People 26

Cities 30

Transportation 34

Natural Resources. 36

Industry 38

Sports. 40

Entertainment 42

Timeline. 44

Glossary 46

Index 48

THE
GRAND CANYON
STATE

Arizona is nestled deep in the nation's Southwest. It is a state filled with natural beauty, including towering red-rock mesas, breathtakingly deep canyons, scorching cactus-filled deserts, and vast tracts of green forests. Even more impressive are Arizona's people and their rich history.

Arizona is a land where legends of the Old West meet the modern world. It is a place where cowboy hats and jingly spurs coexist with factories and skyscrapers. The land dominates everyday life. Arizonans are as familiar with the sun-blasted Sonoran Desert or the Grand Canyon as they are playing a round of golf in a Phoenix suburb. All this diversity is tied together by a love of Southwest cuisine, a spicy blend of Spanish, Mexican, and Native American recipes.

Arizona is a young state. In 1912, it became the last of the contiguous 48 states to join the Union. Today, whether people come to mine, to farm, or run a business—or just for the clean air— millions have found Arizona to be a great place to call home.

Arizona's Grand Canyon.

QUICK FACTS

Name: The word Arizona may be a Spanish variation of a Native American word (*arizonac*) that means "place of little springs."

State Capital: Phoenix, population 1,537,058

Date of Statehood: February 14, 1912 (48th state)

Population: 6,731,484 (15th-most populous state)

Area (Total Land and Water): 113,990 square miles (295,233 sq km), 6th-largest state

Largest City: Phoenix, population 1,537,058

Nicknames: The Grand Canyon State; the Copper State

Motto: *Ditat deus* (God Enriches)

State Bird: Cactus Wren

State Flower: Saguaro Cactus Flower

State Gem: Turquoise

State Tree: Palo Verde

Palo Verde

State Songs: "Arizona March Song" and "Arizona"

Highest Point: Humphreys Peak, 12,637 feet (3,852 m)

Lowest Point: Colorado River, 70 feet (21 m)

Average July High Temperature: 106°F (41°C) in Phoenix in the south; 82°F (28°C) in Flagstaff in the north.

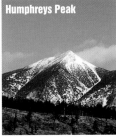
Humphreys Peak

Record High Temperature: 128°F (53°C), at Lake Havasu City, on June 29, 1994.

Average January Low Temperature: 46°F (8°C) in Phoenix in the south; 17°F (-8°C) in Flagstaff in the north.

Record Low Temperature: -40°F (-40°C), at Hawley Lake, on January 7, 1971.

Colorado River

Average Annual Precipitation: 12.4 inches (31.5 cm)

Number of U.S. Senators: 2

Number of U.S. Representatives: 9

U.S. Postal Service Abbreviation: AZ

GEOGRAPHY

Arizona is the 6th-largest state. It measures 113,990 square miles (295,233 sq km) in area. Bordering Arizona to the west are California and Nevada. On the state's east side is New Mexico. Utah is to the north. To the south are the Mexican states of Sonora and Baja. The Colorado River runs between Arizona and southern Nevada, California, and Baja, Mexico.

Arizona's southern half (plus a narrow strip along the state's western edge) includes the Basin and Range Province. This is where most of Arizona's major cities are located, including Phoenix, Tucson, and Kingman. This region is mostly hot and dry. Steep mountain ranges rise up from the surrounding flat desert. Atop the mountains are plants and animals that thrive in the cooler climate.

The McDowell Mountains lie northeast of Phoenix, Arizona. The mountains rise up more than 4,000 feet (1,219 m) from the flat Verde River Basin.

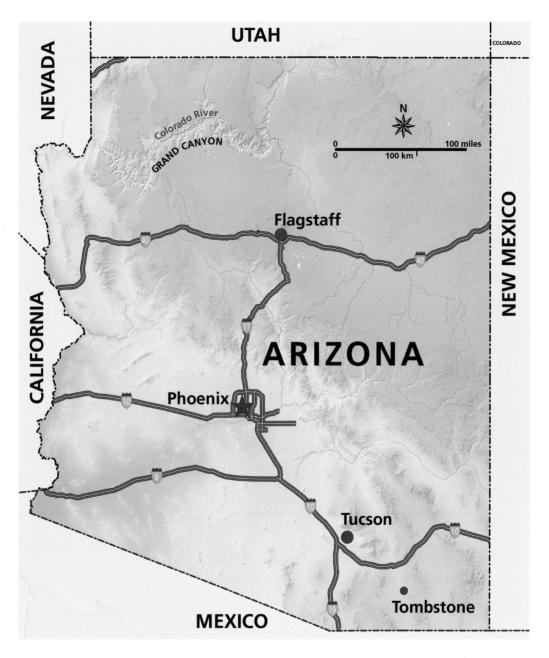

Arizona's total land and water area is
113,990 square miles (295,233 sq km).
It is the 6th-largest state. The state capital is Phoenix.

A cholla cactus thrives in the dry conditions of the Sonoran Desert.

On the scorching southern desert plains, hardy plants and animals such as saguaro cacti and Gila monsters eke out survival in a land that sees very little rain. Sprawling cities depend on underground aquifers and water diverted from the Colorado River.

Major deserts in this region include the Sonoran Desert in the southwestern part of the state, the Mojave Desert to the northwest, and the Chihuahuan Desert in a small part of southeastern Arizona.

A sunbeam shines down illuminating the beauty of a section of the erosion-carved Antelope Canyon.

Arizona's northern half is a flat, semi-arid high country called the Colorado Plateau. Many parts of this region get enough rain for huge forests of ponderosa pine trees to grow. Much of the area, however, is barren rock, carved by erosion into canyons, buttes, and other natural wonders. Spectacular examples can be found around the city of Sedona, the Painted Desert, Antelope Canyon, and the Grand Canyon.

Located in the northern part of the state, the Grand Canyon is Arizona's most famous landmark. Beyond its rim is a great abyss nearly one mile (1.6 km) deep and in some places 18 miles (29 km) across. Carved over millions of years by the Colorado River, the canyon stretches east and west for 277 miles (446 km). The official national park boundary holds about 1.2 million acres (485,623 hectares) of protected wilderness.

GEOGRAPHY

CLIMATE AND WEATHER

Arizona is an arid state, and one of the sunniest in the country. It averages just 12 inches (30 cm) of rain each year. Less than 3 inches (8 cm) falls on the desert areas of the state's southwestern corner. In the winter, when moisture-laden storms from the Pacific Ocean blow over the state, the high elevations in central and northern Arizona can experience heavy snows.

Southern Arizona is mostly desert. Mild winters give way to long, hot summers. The average July high temperature in the Phoenix area is 106°F (41°C). Arizona's record high temperature was 128°F (53°C), at Lake Havasu City, in the Mojave Desert, on June 29, 1994.

Many people live in Phoenix because of its sunny weather. However, summer high temperatures can be brutal, regularly reaching 100°F (38°C) or more.

A rainstorm over the Grand Canyon during the summer monsoon season.

In July and August, Arizona experiences its monsoon season. Warm, moisture-laden air from the Gulf of Mexico can bring dust storms and violent afternoon thunderstorms. Much of the state receives more than half its annual rainfall during this time.

CLIMATE AND WEATHER

PLANTS AND ANIMALS

Saguaro Cactus Blossoms

More than half of Arizona is desert, but there are huge areas of forests and grasslands in the state, especially in the higher elevations on the Colorado Plateau to the north. More than 25 percent of Arizona is forestland. Trees found here include ponderosa pine, Douglas fir, spruce, and aspen.

Many large animals live in Arizona's northern region, and in mountain "islands," which are cooler and wetter than the surrounding desert. These include black bear, deer, antelope, and elk. Other animals found throughout the state include bobcats, coyotes, and mountain lions.

A coyote searches for prey in an Arizona desert.

Saguaro cacti are slow-growing, but may reach 70 feet (21 m) tall over the course of their 150- to 200-year life span.

Many types of cacti grow in the desert. These spiny plants store water in their stems. Giant saguaro cacti are found in the Sonoran Desert in southern Arizona. They are the largest cactus species in the United States. They can grow up to 70 feet (21 m) tall, soak up to 200 gallons (757 l) of rainwater, and live for up to 200 years. The white saguaro blossom is Arizona's state flower.

Mesquite Tree

Javelina

Horned Lizard

Mesquite trees are commonly found in Arizona deserts. They have very long roots that soak up underground water. Saltbrush and sagebrush are common shrubs. Arizona's state tree is the beautiful palo verde.

Small animals found in Arizona's deserts include porcupines, skunks, foxes, and javelinas, which many mistake for wild pigs. They are actually part of the peccary family, which are hoofed mammals that migrated from South America.

Arizona is famous for its desert reptiles. These include rattlesnakes, Arizona coral snakes, desert tortoises, horned lizards, and Gila monsters. Thirteen species of rattlesnakes live in Arizona, the most of any state. The western diamondback is the largest. It grows up to 5.5 feet (1.7 m) long. These poisonous snakes eat animals such as mice and small birds. Their bite is very painful. Fortunately, less than one percent of rattlesnake bites on humans results in death.

Rattlesnake

Roadrunner

Because of its lightning quickness, the roadrunner is one of the few desert dwellers that preys upon rattlesnakes. Using its wings to distract the reptile, the roadrunner will snatch the snake by its tail and snap its head repeatedly against the ground.

Many kinds of birds are found throughout Arizona. They are especially plentiful in the southern part of the state. Game birds include turkeys, quail, and doves. Raptors help keep the state's rodent population under control. These hunters include eagles, falcons, red-tailed hawks, Harris's hawks, great horned owls, and burrowing owls.

Swimming in Arizona's rivers are Colorado pikeminnow (squawfish), several species of suckers, desert pupfish, trout, bass, and catfish. The Apache trout is a native trout species and the official state fish.

HISTORY

Humans first migrated to the desert Southwest as long as 20,000 years ago. In the Arizona area, they included people from the Hohokam, Mogollon, Anasazi, and Salado cultures. The Anasazi are famous for their stone cliff dwellings.

In the 1500s, Spain began sending expeditions into its New World territories. They were searching for riches, including the fabled Seven Cities of Gold. In 1539, Franciscan friar Marcos de Niza traveled north from Mexico City, passing through Arizona on his journey. When he returned, he reported finding a city made of pure gold.

Some Arizona Native Americans lived in cliff dwellings.

Francisco Coronado explored the desert Southwest beginning in 1540. He led more than 300 soldiers for two years. They discovered many amazing wonders, but no gold.

In 1540, Spanish explorer Francisco Vázquez de Coronado led hundreds of conquistadors into the desert Southwest. They discovered the Grand Canyon, the Colorado River, and even ventured as far as the Great Plains in present-day Kansas. Many Native American tribes were encountered, but no gold was found.

For the next 200 years, Arizona was visited by Spanish priests and missionaries. They built a series of missions to bring Christianity to the Native Americans, and to establish centers of trade and ranching. Jesuit priest Eusebio Francisco Kino founded Tumacácori Mission in 1691, north of Nogales.

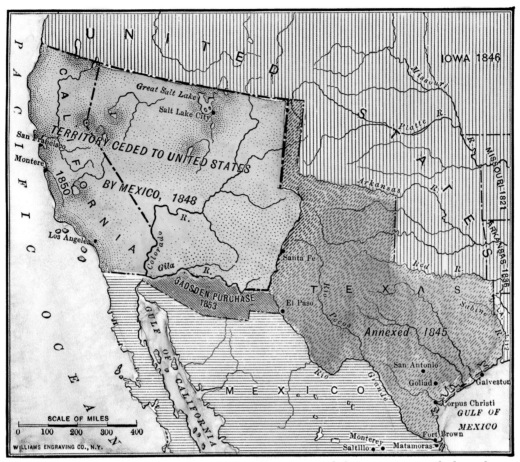

The Gadsden Purchase in 1853, as well as part of the territory ceded to the United States by Mexico in 1848, completed Arizona's current boundary.

Mexico declared independence from Spain in 1821. It kept its vast territories, including modern-day Arizona. In 1846, Mexico and the United States went to war. The cause was a dispute over the southern border of the new state of Texas. When the Mexican-American War ended in 1848, the victorious Americans forced Mexico to give up or sell huge areas of land, nearly one-third of the country. These territories included California, Texas, Nevada, Utah, most of Arizona, New Mexico, and parts of Colorado and Wyoming. The Gadsden Purchase in 1853 completed the rest of Arizona's current boundary.

Following the murder of his wife, mother, and three children by soldiers, Geronimo fought for nearly 35 years against the invasion of Apache lands.

After the war, American settlers poured into the new territory. They included prospectors, farmers, ranchers, adventurers, and businesspeople. The U.S. Army built forts to protect people settling in Arizona or passing through on their way to California. Despite the forts, the military struggled to control violence in the territory.

Many Native American tribes fought fiercely to hold back the tide of American settlers. They refused to be relocated onto reservation land. Led by warriors such as Cochise, Mangas Coloradas, Geronimo, and others, the Apache people fought battles against settlers and the U.S. military for almost 35 years. The Apache Wars finally eased in 1886 after Geronimo's surrender.

A train passes over Canyon Diablo, Arizona, in 1908.

Railroads arrived in Arizona in the 1880s. They connected cities such as St. Louis, Missouri, and New Orleans, Louisiana, with major cities in California. Arizona communities grew near the railroad stops.

Many prospectors struck it rich—and many went bust—searching for copper, gold, and silver under Arizona's rocky crust. Other pioneers made their fortunes ranching, farming, or starting businesses.

Arizona's sudden growth caused problems. Cattle ranchers and sheepherders often fought bloody gun battles over grazing and water rights. Criminals plagued many of the boom towns that sprang up near the mines.

Actors recreate the gunfight at the O.K. Corral in Tombstone, Arizona.

On October 26, 1881, in the town of Tombstone, Marshal Virgil Earp and his brothers Morgan and Wyatt, plus Doc Holliday, squared off against cowboys of the Clanton Gang. They fought in an alley near the O.K. Corral. When the smoke cleared, the cowboys were defeated. The 30-second battle became the most famous shoot-out of the American Old West.

By the 1900s, Arizona had outgrown its lawless past. Cotton and citrus fruits became cash crops. They joined cattle, copper, and climate as the "Five C's," major forces that drove the state's economy. On February 14, 1912, Arizona became the 48th state.

The invention of air conditioning in the 1950s made Arizona a more livable place during the hot summer months. This made the state's population boom. Arizona also became a popular retirement destination.

DID YOU KNOW?

Summer Time   Standard Time

- Arizona has the longest continuously run professional football franchise in the United States. The Cardinals were established in 1898.

- Arizona does not observe daylight saving time in the summer months, except for the Navajo Nation Native American reservation. The only other state that does not observe daylight saving time is Hawaii.

- There are 22 sovereign Native American communities in Arizona. The largest reservation is the Navajo Nation. Most of it is in the northeastern corner of the state. Other Arizona tribes include the Apache, Hopi, Tohono O'odham, Hualapai, Yavapai, Paiute, Zuni, and others. Reservations cover about 25 percent of Arizona. Native Americans represent about 5 percent of the state's total inhabitants.

- One of the biggest meteor craters on Earth lies near the center of Arizona. About 50,000 years ago, an asteroid struck the Earth with the force of 2.5 million tons (2.3 million metric tons) of TNT. Today, Meteor Crater (also called Barringer Crater) can be found near the town of Winslow, Arizona. It is almost 1 mile (1.6 km) wide and 570 feet (174 m) deep.

- During World War II, the United States Marine Corps recruited Navajo Indians from Arizona to send and receive radio messages. The Navajo language is very difficult to learn. Enemy Japanese soldiers were unable to decode the secret radio transmissions. The Navajo Code Talkers saved many American lives.

PEOPLE

John McCain (1936-) is a senior Republican senator from Arizona. He graduated from the United States Naval Academy in 1958. As a naval aviator, McCain flew missions during the Vietnam War. His plane was shot down in  1967. He was a prisoner of war for more than five years. He earned many medals, including the Silver Star and Purple Heart. In 1981, McCain moved to Phoenix, Arizona, and began his long career in politics. He won election to the U.S. House of Representatives in 1982, and the U.S. Senate in 1986. He took over the seat of popular Arizona conservative Barry Goldwater. To date, McCain has served for five straight terms in the U.S. Senate. In 2008, he unsuccessfully ran for president against Barack Obama.

Cochise (1815?-1874) was a Native American chief of the Chiricahua Apache tribe. His people respected his bravery and honesty. But he could also be cruel to his enemies. Along with other Indian leaders such as Mangas Coloradas and Geronimo, he fought to defend his homeland. By the mid-1800s, Mexican and American settlers wanted to drive the Apache off their lands. Cochise kept the peace with the Americans until 1861, when he was falsely accused of cattle rustling and kidnapping. Cochise spent the next decade fighting. He finally surrendered in 1872. He spent the final two years of his life on an Arizona reservation.

Sandra Day O'Connor (1930-) became the first woman to serve on the United States Supreme Court in 1981. She was born in El Paso, Texas, but grew up on a cattle ranch near Duncan, Arizona. In 1952, she graduated near the top of her class at Stanford Law School. In the late 1960s and early 1970s, O'Connor served in the Arizona Senate. She then became a judge in Maricopa County, near Phoenix. In 1981, she was appointed to the U.S. Supreme Court by President Ronald Reagan. O'Connor served on the Supreme Court until her retirement in 2006.

Astronomer **Percival Lowell** (1855-1916) built Lowell Observatory in Flagstaff, Arizona, in 1894. Although born and educated in Cambridge, Massachusetts, Lowell spent many years in his Arizona observatory. He made early maps of Mars and Venus. Lowell thought he detected canals built by an ancient civilization on Mars. Although later proven false, Lowell's claim fired the public's imagination and made them interested in astronomy.

Author Stephenie Meyer became famous for her Twilight *series of books, which were published from 2005 to 2008. She also wrote the science fiction book* The Host *in 2008. All of these books have been made into movies.*

Stephenie Meyer (1973-) is the best-selling author of the popular *Twilight* series of books about vampires, werewolves, and young romance. The books have sold more than 100 million copies worldwide. Meyer was born in Hartford, Connecticut, but grew up in Phoenix, Arizona. The idea for *Twilight* came to her in a dream in 2003. She had little writing experience, but set out to tell her tale anyway. She completed the novel in just three months.

CITIES

Phoenix is the capital of Arizona. It is the state's largest city. It has a population of 1,537,058. It is the center of a large metropolitan area called the Valley of the Sun, which includes suburbs such as Mesa, Tempe, Scottsdale, and Glendale. Together, the metro area contains more than four million people. Phoenix was established in 1868 by farmers who used canals to bring water to the parched land, something Native Americans had done centuries earlier. Agriculture is still important to the city today, but it has been surpassed by high tech and service industries. Phoenix became the state capital in 1912, the same year Arizona gained statehood. Arizona State University has a campus in the city.

Tucson (TOO sahn) is one of the oldest cities in the United States. It is located in the Sonoran Desert and is surrounded by five mountain ranges. It is Arizona's second-largest city, with a population of 527,972. Spanish missionaries first visited the Tucson area in the late 1600s. The word "Tucson" is a variation of a Pima Native American term that means "water at the foot of black mountain." Tucson has a rich cultural heritage, with Spanish, Mexican, Anglo-American, and Native American influences. It has a small-town atmosphere but big-city resources. Outdoor lovers flock to Tucson for biking, skiing, and golf. The University of Arizona and Davis-Monthan Air Force Base are major employers.

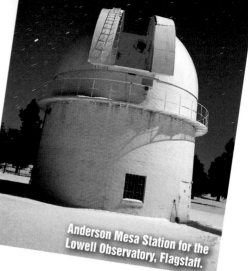

Anderson Mesa Station for the Lowell Observatory, Flagstaff.

Flagstaff is located in the north-central part of Arizona. Its elevation of 7,000 feet (2,134 m) keeps temperatures cooler than in the southern deserts. First settled in 1876, Flagstaff is nestled at the base of the San Francisco Peaks. The largest ponderosa pine forest in the country is nearby. During the city's early years, lumber was an important part of the economy. Flagstaff's population today is 68,785. Northern Arizona University and Coconino Community College are located in Flagstaff. At Lowell Observatory, astronomers discovered the dwarf planet Pluto. In addition to government services, transportation, and education, tourism is an important industry in Flagstaff. Many people stop here on their way to the Grand Canyon.

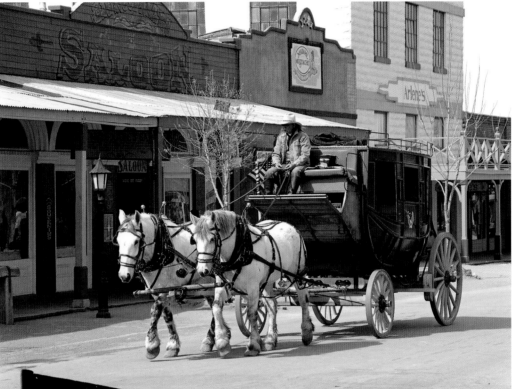

Tombstone, with a population of just 1,322, is a small town with a lot of history. It was one of the most well known of Arizona's early mining camps. Prospector Ed Schieffelin was once told that the only stone he would find would be his own tombstone. After discovering a rich vein of silver, he decided to name his mine Tombstone. The name passed on to the town when it was founded in 1879. When the silver mines finally ran out, the population began to dwindle. But, as its motto declares, Tombstone was a "town too tough to die." Famous as the site of the October 26, 1881, shoot-out near the O.K. Corral, Tombstone today is a popular tourist destination.

TRANSPORTATION

More than 66,000 miles (106,217 km) of roads crisscross Arizona. Many follow former wagon train roads. These roads in turn traced pioneer trails and Native American trade routes. The main interstate highways in Arizona are I-40, I-8, and I-10. They generally run east and west. I-19 and I-17 run north and south, while I-15 cuts across the northwest corner of the state.

Railroads played an important part in Arizona's growth. They arrived in the 1880s to transport goods and settlers. Today, freight and passenger trains still chug across the Arizona landscape. Amtrak serves most major Arizona cities outside the Phoenix area.

A container train carries goods across Arizona.

Phoenix Sky Harbor International Airport

Arizona's biggest airport is Phoenix Sky Harbor International Airport. It is one of the busiest airports in the world. It serves more than 110,000 fliers daily. Other major airports include Tucson International Airport, Phoenix-Mesa Gateway Airport, Yuma International Airport, and Flagstaff Pulliam Airport. Many tourists fly to Grand Canyon National Park Airport.

The Grand Canyon National Park Airport is only 7 miles (11 km) from the South Rim of the Grand Canyon. It is Arizona's 4th busiest airport.

TRANSPORTATION

NATURAL RESOURCES

Mining has long been important to Arizona's economy. The state has been the country's main copper producer for more than 100 years. Other minerals dug from Arizona mines include zinc, uranium, and

Copper Ore

coal. A small amount of oil is drilled in the state's northeastern corner.

Because so much of the state is desert, many people don't think of agriculture when they think of Arizona. However, thanks to effective irrigation, many major crops are grown year-round. Top crops include lettuce, hay, cotton, citrus fruits, alfalfa, nuts, honeydew melons, and apples. Arizona grows enough cotton annually to make at least one pair of jeans for every person in the United States.

Lettuce thrives in an irrigated Arizona farm field.

A cattle ranch in Arizona.

About one million head of cattle roam Arizona's rangeland. Other important livestock are sheep and poultry. Timber is harvested in the vast forests of the north.

Perhaps Arizona's most important natural resource is water. In a land with limited groundwater and a booming population, clean water is critical. Arizona tightly manages the flow of its streams and rivers, balancing the need for drinking water versus crop irrigation. The mining industry also requires water. These competing needs sometimes cause disputes, even between Arizona and neighboring states.

NATURAL RESOURCES

INDUSTRY

Arizona has a large economy, bigger than Ireland or New Zealand. In the past, the state was dependent on the "Five Cs"—copper, cotton, cattle, citrus, and climate. Copper was Arizona's most important industry from 1880 to 1950. Even today, more than half of the country's copper is mined in Arizona. In fact, the state flag features a copper-colored star in the middle to remind people of the metal's importance.

Although mining remains a leading Arizona industry, manufacturing

Trucks haul ore out of the open-pit Morenci Mine in Morenci, Arizona. It is the largest copper mine in North America and one of the largest in the world.

is even more important today. Arizona factories make many things, from food products to electronics. Phoenix and Tucson are key manufacturing centers. Other industries that bring jobs and money to the state include finance, aerospace, transportation, health services, logging, farming, and cattle.

Monument Valley

Tourism has become very important to Arizona. In 2013, about 34 million people visited the state, adding almost $40 billion to the economy. Arizona has many national parks and monuments, including the Grand Canyon, Meteor Crater, Monument Valley, Lake Powell, the Painted Desert, and Petrified Forest. The state's historical sites, such as the Old West town of Tombstone, are also popular destinations.

Petrified Forest

SPORTS

Arizona hosts several professional sports teams. The Arizona Cardinals play in the National Football League. The Phoenix Suns are in the National Basketball Association. The Phoenix Mercury play in the Women's National Basketball Association. The Mercury won the WNBA Finals in 2007, 2009, and 2014. The Arizona Coyotes play in the National Hockey League. The Arizona Diamondbacks are a Major League Baseball team. The Diamondbacks won the World Series in 2001. The Arizona Rattlers are an Arena Football League team with five championship wins. Arizona United SC is a member of the United Soccer League.

Arizonans also love college sports. The University of Arizona Wildcats (located in Tucson) and the Arizona State Sun Devils (in Tempe) are longtime rivals, competing against each other since the late 1880s. Their annual football matchup is called the "Duel in the Desert."

Outdoor lovers can find all kinds of activities in Arizona. The state has many golf courses, bike trails, and even ski resorts in the mountains. Hiking is popular in Arizona's national parks and monuments. Many people also enjoy camping, hunting, and river rafting.

A snowboarder rides at
Arizona Snowbowl in Flagstaff.

People enjoy rafting on the wild
Colorado River in the Grand Canyon.

SPORTS

ENTERTAINMENT

The Phoenix area has some of the finest museums in the Southwest. The Heard Museum features the art and history of Native American and Hispanic culture. The Phoenix Art Museum displays classical and modern art from all around the world. The city also is home to the Children's Museum of Phoenix, the Arizona Science Center, and the unique Musical Instrument Museum, which displays rare instruments from cultures around the world.

A Native American performs in the Heard Museum's Annual World Championship Hoop Dance Contest in Phoenix, Arizona.

The San Xavier del Bac Mission is called the "White Dove of the Desert." Construction of the buildings began in 1783. Rising out of the desert, the mission can be seen for miles.

Arizona has a thriving musical scene, with heavy Mexican-American influences. Phoenix is a center of rock music. It is also home to the Phoenix Symphony Orchestra. The city of Tucson hosts the Tucson Symphony Orchestra. It performs classical music as well as jazz, folk, and mariachi.

Native American art can be found throughout Arizona. Hopi and Navajo artists create many kinds of popular artwork including paintings, jewelry, blankets, and pottery.

Arizona's long and colorful history produced many Spanish colonial-style buildings. Mission San Xavier del Bac, south of Tucson, was built between 1783-1797. Called the "White Dove of the Desert" for its striking stucco walls, it is one of the most photographed buildings in the state, hosting about 200,000 visitors each year.

TIMELINE

1100-1500—Apache, Hopi, and Navajo tribes live in the area that will become Arizona.

1539—Marcos de Niza explores the area, looking for gold.

1540-1542—Francisco Vázquez de Coronado leads a group of people into Arizona, exploring the state and seeking riches.

1846-1848—The Mexican-American War is fought. The United States takes over ownership of land that will become Arizona.

1853—The United States buys the remaining part of Arizona, the area south of Phoenix.

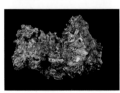

1854—Copper is discovered in Arizona.

1863—Arizona becomes a territory of the United States. John Noble Goodwin is appointed governor.

1912—Arizona becomes the 48th state in the Union.

Grand Canyon National Park 1919

1919—The Grand Canyon becomes Arizona's first national park.

1942-1945—Navajo Code Talkers serve with the U.S. Marines in World War II.

2001—The Arizona Diamondbacks baseball team wins the World Series.

2008—Arizona Republican Senator John McCain unsuccessfully runs for president. He continues serving the state of Arizona in the U.S. Senate.

2015—The NFL's 49th Super Bowl is played at University of Phoenix Stadium in Glendale, Arizona, on February 1. The New England Patriots beat the Seattle Seahawks 28-24.

GLOSSARY

ABYSS

A deep hole or opening in the ground, often so deep it appears bottomless.

APACHE

A Native American tribe that lived in Arizona before Europeans arrived. They fiercely fought to defend and keep their homeland from white settlers.

AQUIFER

Water that is underground, in the dirt and rock. Unlike an underground river in a cave, an aquifer is water that is saturated in the ground—like a kitchen sponge. Water can be pumped out for irrigation and other uses.

ARID

A very dry climate.

CONQUISTADORS

Spanish military men who explored the New World and conquered many of the Indian tribes living in the Americas.

MARCOS DE NIZA

A Spanish explorer who traveled through the Arizona area in 1539.

MARIACHI

A street band whose members dress in traditional Mexican clothing and often walk about playing rhythmic Spanish folk music.

MONSOON

A wind that lasts a long time, even for weeks or months. Summer months are monsoon season in Arizona.

Navajo

A group of Native Americans that live primarily in Arizona, New Mexico, and Utah. They are known for their work with livestock, as well as creating beautiful weavings, pottery, and silver jewelry.

New World

The areas of North, Central, and South America, as well as islands near these land masses. The term was often used by European explorers.

Plateau

A large, flat section of land that is raised up from the surrounding countryside. This area of high ground is mostly flat at the top.

Raptor

Birds of prey that eat meat, such as eagles, falcons, hawks, and owls.

Sovereign

A government that is free to make its own rules without outside interference.

Vietnam War

A conflict between the countries of North Vietnam and South Vietnam from 1954-1975. Communist North Vietnam was supported by China and the Soviet Union. The United States entered the war on the side of South Vietnam.

World War II

A conflict that was fought from 1939 to 1945, involving countries around the world. The United States entered the war after Japan bombed the American naval base at Pearl Harbor, in Oahu, Hawaii, on December 7, 1941.

INDEX

A

Amtrak 34
Anasazi 18
Antelope Canyon 11
Apache 21, 24, 27
Apache Wars 21
Arena Football League 40
Arizona Cardinals 40
Arizona Coyotes 40
Arizona Diamondbacks 40
Arizona Rattlers 40
Arizona Science Center 42
Arizona State University 30, 40
Arizona United SC 40
Army, U.S. 21

B

Baja, Mexico 8
Barringer Crater 25 (*see also* Meteor Crater)
Basin and Range Province 8

C

California 8, 20, 21, 22
Cambridge, MA 28
Cardinals (football franchise) 24
Chihuahuan Desert 10
Children's Museum of Phoenix 42
Chiricahua Apache 27
Christianity 19
Clanton Gang 23
Cochise 21, 27
Coconino Community College 32
Colorado 20
Colorado Plateau 11, 14
Colorado River 8, 10, 11, 19
Connecticut 29
Coronado, Francisco Vázquez de 19

D

Davis-Monthan Air Force Base 31
Duel in the Desert 40
Duncan, AZ 28

E

Earp, Morgan 23
Earp, Virgil 23
Earp, Wyatt 23
Earth 25
El Paso, TX 28

F

Five C's 23, 38
Flagstaff, AZ 28, 32
Flagstaff Pulliam Airport 35

G

Gadsden Purchase 20
Geronimo 21, 27
Glendale, AZ 30
Goldwater, Barry 26
Grand Canyon 4, 11, 19, 32, 39
Grand Canyon National Park Airport 35
Great Plains 19
Gulf of Mexico 13

H

Hartford, CT 29
Hawaii 24
Heard Museum 42
Hohokam 18
Holliday, Doc 23
Hopi 24, 43
House of Representatives, U.S. 26
Hualapai 24

I

Ireland 38

J

Jesuit 19

K

Kansas 19
Kingman, AZ 8
Kino, Eusebio Francisco 19

L

Lake Havasu City, AZ 12
Louisiana 22
Lowell, Percival 28
Lowell Observatory 28, 32

M

Major League Baseball 40
Mangas Coloradas 21, 27
Maricopa County 28
Marine Corps, U.S. 25
Mars 28
Massachusetts 28
McCain, John 26
Mesa, AZ 30
Meteor Crater 25, 39
Mexican-American War 20
Mexico 8, 20
Mexico City, Mexico 18

Meyer, Stephenie 29
Mission San Xavier del Bac 43
Missouri 22
Mogollon 18
Mojave Desert 10, 12
Monument Valley 39
Musical Instrument Museum 42

N

National Basketball Association 40
National Football League 40
National Hockey League 40
Navajo (language) 25
Navajo Code Talkers 25
Navajo Indians 25, 43
Navajo Nation 24
Nevada 8, 20
New Mexico 8, 20
New Orleans, LA 22
New World 18
New Zealand 38
Niza, Marcos de 18
Nogales, AZ 19
Northern Arizona University 32

O

Obama, Barack 26
O'Connor, Sandra Day 28
O.K. Corral 23, 33
Old West 4, 23, 39

P

Pacific Ocean 12
Painted Desert 11, 39
Paiute 24
Petrified Forest 39
Phoenix, AZ 4, 8, 12, 26, 28, 29, 30, 34, 38, 42, 43
Phoenix Art Museum 42
Phoenix Mercury 40
Phoenix Sky Harbor International Airport 35
Phoenix Suns 40
Phoenix Symphony Orchestra 43
Phoenix-Mesa Gateway Airport 35
Pima 31
Pluto 32
Powell, Lake 39
Purple Heart (medal) 26

R

Reagan, Ronald 28

S

Salado 18
San Francisco Peaks 32
Schieffelin, Ed 33

Scottsdale, AZ 30
Sedona, AZ 11
Senate, Arizona 28
Senate, U.S. 26
Seven Cities of Gold 18
Silver Star (medal) 26
Sonora, Mexico 8
Sonoran Desert 4, 10, 15, 31
South America 16
Southwest 4, 18, 19, 42
Spain 18, 20
St. Louis, MO 22
Stanford Law School 28
Sun Devils 40
Supreme Court, U.S. 28

T

Tempe, AZ 30, 40
Texas 20, 28
Tohono O'odham 24
Tombstone (mine) 33
Tombstone, AZ 23, 33, 39
Tucson, AZ 8, 31, 38, 40, 43
Tucson International Airport 35
Tucson Symphony Orchestra 43
Tumacácori Mission 19
Twilight (book series) 29

U

Union 4
United Soccer League 40
United States 15, 20, 21, 24, 26, 28, 31, 36
United States Naval Academy 26
University of Arizona 31, 40
Utah 8, 20

V

Valley of the Sun 30
Venus 28
Vietnam War 26

W

White Dove of the Desert 43
Wildcats 40
Winslow, AZ 25
WNBA Finals 40
Women's National Basketball Association 40
World Series 40
World War II 25
Wyoming 20

Y

Yavapai 24
Yuma International Airport 35

Z

Zuni 24